Loving *Me* Right

Pierre Alex Jeanty

Cover Design: Amy Franke / @afgraphics
Editor: Carla DuPont / @writewithcarla

ISBN-13: 978-1-949191-18-9

For more information, please visit:
Pierrejeanty.com
Contact: contact@jeaniuspublishing.com

This book is not a celebration of one's inability to love, it's a way of expressing the difficulty that comes with falling in love after the wrong hands have held you before.

This airs out the doubts, opens up the fears, and brings insecurities to the forefront, all for the sake of building a better love story.

Loving Me

Unbuttoning the calluses,
slowly undressing my heart for you to see
the naked me,
my true intentions,
the softness inside of me,
the grace flowing,
all of the strength and sacrifices swimming
through me,
everything I am willing to do
for the person who loves me right,
the soul willing to walk the road of patience with
me,
the person whose mouth is full of understanding,
whose heart wants to never forget my name.
I am willing to be naked
as long you are willing to love me as I am.

Putting your heart up for auction
is always a difficult task,
even when the highest bidder
looks everything like love
and is willing to forfeit everything to have you.

I am still feeling it,

the way they made me feel like

the most important person in the world.

Finally, my heart is safe,

I remember my tired mind whispering,

only to be followed by growling sounds

and sheep's skin lying on the floor.

A fool I became again,

lured by a fool looking to cage someone inside

their world and feast on their heart.

This is my broken story.

So, when I meet another person with good

promises and lots of hope in their eyes,

I can't help but wonder if this is another magic

trick

and I'm playing victim again.

There are days when love is easier said than done
and days when the doing is easier than the saying.

When failure and disappointment
have been served to you
more than enough times,
just taking what they bring to the table isn't
enough.

Overanalyzing things
becomes the safest way to engage.

Walking with more fear in your heart
than love starts to become normal.

Love has been a game to me.
One that consists of me being played
while I play the clueless romantic character
with hope in potentials that never had a chance to
blossom.

Love has been a game to me
even when I never saw it in such light.
I've dealt myself some bad hands,
finding myself in the cage of players.
I'm just trying to make sure letting someone else
win my heart isn't another losing situation.

Let's be different from the norm and fight instead of escaping when things don't go our way.

I can only be with someone who likes to preserve things, fix things, and take good care of things.

I am simply afraid.
Afraid of investing more of myself for more
heartaches in return.
Afraid of falling into the wrong arms again.
Afraid of being disappointed by short-lived
promises once again.
Afraid of creating memories I will fight to bury
once again.
Afraid of laying in a bed of lust once again.
Afraid of turning strangers into lovers only for
them to turn back into strangers again.
Afraid of kissing lips that will say 'goodbye' once
again.

I am simply afraid of finding myself back on the
frontline for disappointment.

I was so accustomed to the bare minimum
that guilt was the only thing I felt
when I opened my mouth to ask for more.

If it looks like I am afraid of love,
that's because I am making sure
I never want to meet a lover like the ones I've
loved before or meet a love like what I've
recognized as love.

It's not love that I am afraid of,
or relationships I am running from,
it's the bad relationships I've run into,
in the name of love,
that I don't want to find myself running into
anymore.

The secret to loving me,
is to love me without secrets.

The key to winning my heart,
is to show me the key to yours.

My heart drops at the thought of
offering it to another hand.

Right now,
this is something I cannot do
without my joints locking up
and my bones sweating
as I extend my hand with fingers trembling in fear.

Handing my heart over without breaking it,
like those who hurt me,
seems almost impossible.

Choosing myself no longer feels
like performing an exorcism,
I've made peace with my demons.

Now it feels like love.

When a person finds love for themselves,
accepting the worst while hoping for better
is no longer acceptable.

I will not treat you the way your ex mistreated
you.
So, comparing me to them should
never be a treat I have to taste.

I will never get how letting someone who wants to
love your soul to know the deepest and rawest
things about you firsthand is an unsafe practice
that we shy from.

So many of us trust people to be intimate
physically,
but fear true intimacy.

Some of us are even more willing to whisper our
deepest secrets to a random stranger than to the
stranger auditioning for our heart.

Without honesty,
love is a two-legged bed trying to balance two
bodies.

Anything founded on just enough to stand,
will not stand the test of time.

Love is about going all in.

Let's be friends who tell each other everything,
not just good things.

Let's not just try to make it work.
Trying is dipping your toes to check how cold the
water can get.
Let's make it work.
Choosing to jump in with the mindset that we will
do whatever it takes to stay afloat and thrive.
Let's drown in each other and learn as we go.
Let's become the love stories we've imagined.
Let's build the relationship goals we've idolized.
Let's be the couple we wanted so bad to be with
our exes.
Let's pour all the good and all the bad into this
relationship and let it paint something beautiful.
We don't have to force anything,
but we can work hard to make sure it never ends.

My heart is yours.
I will not try to convince you that it is.
I am only responsible for showing you
without ever opening my mouth.

I am out of cravings for the honeymoon phase,
I want to see who you are on the sour days,
what words come out of your mouth
when the bitter taste of argument is on your
tongue,
how you react to the foul smell of tension between
us,
how you respond to the ugly voice of anger,
I am eager to see the part of you that is hard to
love,
it's the part that will motivate me to love hard.

New love doesn't carry much reward to me
anymore.

It's a pot of risks that look more like consequences
which will swallow my confidence whole at the
end of every heartbreak.

New love may be exciting,
but excitement never shows up when it comes to
solving problems, just how to leave when the
mood is gone.

I love the smell of new love,
but I am allergic to the scent it leaves behind
when it loses its newness.

Can we be friends, first, and truly see that
through?

So many times, it's been a goal of mine,
but I let the butterflies convince me to just go with
the flow.

A current that seems to only take me down the
streams of heartbreak.

What's funny is every single person
I failed to reach this goal with never found reasons
to stay.

This time around, I am not allowing myself to
commit to anyone who can't commit to building a
friendship with me first.

I have plenty of love to give.

It's the way to give it that I am still learning.

How to let it leave me without feeling it has left

me,

is what I am trying to figure out.

I have plenty of love to give,

it's just that I can only pour it slowly.

Anyone is easy to love
when there is nothing but sunshine.
I am asking to be loved when
there's rain,
thunderstorms,
hurricanes, and tsunamis.
I want someone who will be there to watch the
sunrise and rainbows spread their color palette
against the sky.

I've heard that people who need love most do not
ask for it in the most loving ways.
If I am honest, I am trying not to be one of those
people.
I recognize that I do not know my love language.
Everything my heart has learned to hear from
lovers always carries a heavy accent of lies.
My tired ears no longer yearn to interpret the
misinterpretations.
Instead,
I've grown deaf to the voices that are supposed to
be love, afraid of trusting it even when it's coming
from inside of me.

Sincerely, my unloving ways.

I am planting confidence in this flesh of mine.
The last person who fed me promises took too
much of it with them when they packed their
heart and left me with this baggage.
Since then, I've been speaking to God more.
I've been letting self-care raise my awareness,
giving poems room to speak to the deeper part of
me, letting journaling and practicing self-love help
me keep my mirror clean.
I can't say it has come back yet.
I can only say it's finding its way back home.

Teach me to love,
we don't just learn certain things on our own.

When we do,
it's easy for us to assume we are right when we
aren't.

Guessing games
are for those who have time to settle.

I'm out of time,
I want to learn to love you or I'll learn to let go.

What we are is a conversation that should happen
face-to-face before we are
tongue-to-tongue,
body-to-body
or heart-to-heart.

We must crawl before we fall in love.

I believe I am ready to love.

However, I sometimes feel that I may not be ready for love.

But, I am learning to be ready for you.

It's a privilege to be with me,
I say this as humbly as possible.
Just as I believe it's a privilege to be with you.
I've survived too many trips around the sun
to let anyone throw shade and be ungrateful for
my presence in their life.

Sometimes, I shed tears asking myself,
am I enough?
Questioning what is it about me that will make
you stay,
thinking about my imperfections and if they will
guide you to the door.
Will my past convince you to leave me in yours?
Are the scars tattooed on my flesh too much for
you?
Is the battle I am fighting with my past capable of
taking out the future?
There are days I even ask if I am deserving of
more than what I've been served.

I am not a survivor,
my spine is built from perseverance.
I will endure anything just to get to the other side.
I've even persevered through loneliness, both in
the single life and in lifeless relationships.
Persevere with me and I will make sure our
relationship sees the other side.

To some people,

the memories of past love reminds them of the

good times.

It reminds them of the potential

that the relationship once held in its palm.

I've been one of those people,

those days are long gone.

The memories are now what I use

to sniff out the smell of red flags.

Do not tell me what love is supposed to look like.

Do not paint an image of love with just your

words.

Say it to me through the way you love me.

Paint it to me.

Let your character whisper it to me.

I do not want to guess, nor search for it.

Don't say, "*I love you*" to me,

unless you live up to those words.

You see,

not seeing eye-to-eye is a great indicator

we are seeing life through different lenses.

In the past,

I thought this was a sign of the beginning of the

end. Experience taught me that good relationships

are about what two people build while being

themselves.

Let's disagree without being disagreeable

and open each other's eyes in different ways.

I am searching
for more than I've experienced
and by more,
I mean more real
than what I've had.

They say, "**If it's meant to be, it'll be.**"
How can this be true when relationships are
supposed to be hard work?
How can it be when all the love stories I've
allowed to write themselves can't seem to find a
happy ending?
They say, "**Don't judge a book by its cover.**"
Yet, writers invest hours into the book cover
creation process.
Covers are meant to be judged because they give
us an idea of what's printed on the pages.
These cliches only make sense in their setting and
so far, '**fight for love**' has been the only one I find
to be true.
If we want 'it' to be, it'll always be, as long as we
don't stop fighting for it.

Everyone fighting for love isn't fighting for love.
Taking blow after blow to your self-respect, self-
confidence, and your overall well-being to keep
someone who doesn't want to be yours looks
nothing like love.

Unrequited love only looks like love to one person.

Tiptoeing my way
around cupid's missed arrows
has been how my heart gets its cardio.

I will fight for love,
I will only fight for love.
I will not fight for people.
Fighting for people can mean fighting
against love if they do not love you.

Letting go has always been hard for me
whether it's letting go of habits,
letting go of certain behaviors,
or letting go of strangers I once trusted my heart
with.

I don't walk away easily,
not from what hurt me or who hurt me.
Neither will I walk away from you easily.

Time may not heal all wounds but with time,

I am healing.

Over time,

the hinges on the doors of my heart will fall off,

the walls will crumble

and all of me will fall into your hands.

Give me time,

this journey isn't an easy one.

Besides,

I heard patience gives life-changing rewards.

The forever you believe in was once my religion.
I prayed for it and worshipped every thought of it.
I chased it and crowned it the truth that would
enlighten souls.
I craved this paradise, I looked for the angels in
crooked souls.
And that's when it all came crashing down,
when my heart started to feel that believing in a
love this good was a sin.
How can it be when hell became the relationship I
was in?
When my prayers kept falling onto deaf ears,
giving me only wolves in love's clothing.

Pardon me if it seems like I've lost faith.
I am a little jaded, I've been given reason to be.
I am trying to find new reasons to get rid of those
reasons.
I am looking for the miracle happy couples have.
Maybe you are heaven sent, maybe forever can be
found with you.
Time will tell, but now I am letting you know it's
hard to believe in a forever I have yet to see.

If your expectations for me are near perfection,
please don't fall for me.
I am as imperfect as they come.
Sometimes I misplace my anger,
the wrong words sometimes fall from my lips.
I react incorrectly on some occasions and give cold
shoulders even to the people who've given me
their shoulders to lean on.
I am a perfect mess,
that's the only perfect thing about me.
If you're looking for someone near perfect,
you'll break your own heart being with me.

Understanding is sexy,
so is consistency.
Give me those
and watch the way my guard falls
and my mind comes undone.

Promise me that your love will not look like the version of love you received from the people who couldn't love you.

The sweetest hypocrisy that seems to always find a way to thrive is people being the exact version of their ex.

I can be a hypocrite sometimes,
this is me being raw with you.

There are behaviors I stole from people in my
past.
Habits of theirs that became practices of mine,
subconsciously.

When you see those behaviors that I complain
about show up in our love life,
be sure to remind me that the past has no room in
our future.

When I speak bad of my exes,
I am not spewing hate,
I am not making it aware that their scent and their
memories are still hung up on the walls of my
mind.
I am not expressing the sinful thoughts that still
linger here.

When I speak bad of my exes,
I am airing out the bad memories they've given
me.
I am shouting at the experience,
I am practicing hanging up on the past.

Speaking about the bad is sometimes how I
remind myself that I am ready for something good,
that I need something good,
that I have something good, with you.

I am not talking about my ex, I am talking bad
about the **EX**periences while trying to make room
for new ones.

Depression knocks,
with knuckles full of hardships from this life,
or fistfuls of nightmares that will not leave my
mind vacant.

People never realized all the trauma they've left
me with.
It's not their burden.
Why should it be when I am responsible for me?
Let's not forget that in my story of overcoming,
there are still paragraphs and chapters about
things I've had to overcome.
Sometimes those parts find a way to come over,
to have drinks with my pain,
and laugh about my healing journey,
a mockery that rips smiles out of my face and
sinks relationships.

When my lips find the strength to tell you
all I've been through,
please know I am not a victim,
have empathy for me,
but keep sympathy from joining the party.

I want to say 'I love you' last.
Putting love first has never been where I fall short.
The problem is letting it fly out of my mouth
without wings and proper hands to catch it.
The outcome has always been rewarding deaf ears
with the melody from my heart.

I want to say 'I love you' last, not out of
competition but out of certainty.
I am sure I will love hard.
It's trusting another person to mean those words.
When they say those words, I find it hard to do.
I don't know if you're willing to jump and truly
mean it.
I just don't want to be first unless what we have is
set up to last.

My soul is still letting go of the things I've let go of.

Can you remember what it was like when your
last relationship ended?

Can you remember how the air felt heavy, how
crying came so easily?

Can you remember the pain beating against your
heartbeat?

Can you remember how it felt when someone said
you'd find better and it felt like a punch to the gut?

Your thoughts whispered about the perks of a
single life.

Can you remember?

Because I still can and trying to forget is most of
my battle.

I am not cold.
It takes me a long time to warm up to people now.
I am numb.
I am cautious.
I procrastinate when it comes to dating.
I am full of doubts.

I am not cold.
I'm just slow to jump in the fire after it has burnt
so many bridges in my life.

I don't have the answers as to why I question us,
why I question you,
why I act like good things don't deserve me.
I don't have the answers, but I am full of questions.
Like, why did your eyes pick me?
What will our journey look like five years from
now?
Will you leave when things get tough?
Which argument will be our last?
I know you don't have the answers, but time will
tell.

Are you here to fight,

to stand in the cage love placed us in to swing our

tired arms and defend our bruised hearts?

Are you here to be my left hook when nothing is

going right for me?

Because I'm here to throw my right when you feel

like you have nothing left.

Are you here to take jabs at the opinions, the

doubts, the ugly things and everything meant to

stop us?

Are you here to fight me or fight with me?

When you spot certain behaviors
or habits that sink their teeth into the good thing
we have going on,
nip it in the bud.
I may be learning to accept criticism from those
still learning me,
but I will always come to my senses when it's for
something good.

After years of getting the finger pointed
at my insecurities
in the name of constructive criticism,
I've learned to point first
and listen
to comprehend later.

When correction has been used
as a gun to shoot you down
by people who are unwilling
to make changes themselves,
anything close to it often looks like a weapon.

I cannot wait for these fears to fall off,
for trust to show up in every part of our
relationship.
I can't wait for these doubts to disappear,
fade into our past.
I can't wait to comfortably listen to your heart.
I can't wait to genuinely connect soul-to-soul with
you.

Please don't give my silence a voice without my
permission
This is how assumption uses its gossiping tongue
to poison what is meant to be.
Let my silence be just what it is
and assumptions be in charge of participating in
the minor things that will never reroute our love,
our bond, us.

The nightmares I have about love
come from stories I never told.

Stories I promise to tell you when what we have is
settled,
when certainty has enough room in our
relationship,
when we are established.

And what we have looks nothing
like a dream but a reality I've dreamed about.

I prefer consistency over loyalty.

Don't get me wrong,

I want you to be loyal to us the way I plan on being

loyal to you,

but until you're consistent I cannot trust it.

I've had enough encounters with those too loyal to

inconsistency.

When you're committed and consistent at building

us, loyalty will become undeniable.

You not ghosting me like the others, spoke to me.
I am not treating crumbs as a full course meal.
I'm just grateful that we swam shallow waters in
this terrible dating pool.

If those failed relationships taught me anything,
it's that loving people who aren't willing to love
you is draining.
It's watching someone drink every drop of
happiness from you with the straw you gifted
them.
Or watching them stab your heart with the knife
you gifted them to cut ties with their past.

If those failed relationships taught me anything,
it's that I am guilty of giving them power just as
they are guilty of abusing it.

There will be things I cry about that don't deserve
a tear and things that deserve every ounce of
water out of me,
yet will not get a tear from me.
I'll apologize for being too emotional and too
unemotional at times.
When the line has been blurred between real and
fake so much in your life,
it leaves you out of touch.
I am both numb and over sensitive,
This is who I am,
I am learning to differentiate between what's good
for me and what's been bad to me.
All I am asking is for you to be soft with me, even
when you must be hard on me.

I am a turtle when it comes to the race of love.
Being slow is the least reason I call myself that.
Having an outer shell that I use to fend off people I
think are predators while being a softy on the
inside is why.

I am a turtle, slow with a scute over my heart,
because pain has stabbed me far too many times.

It's not privacy that I hate,
it's becoming a secret that has to be kept,
having a relationship that is just a whisper
or dressing up like a clown without recognizing
something funny is going on.
It's secrecy that I don't like at all.

I am not asking for you to put up with me,
I simply want you to be here
while I put things down
that have held me up
for far too long.

Break my heart, instead of breaking my trust.

Heartbreak is easier when it's alone without a
shot of betrayal to wash down as well.

"We didn't work out," is never a bad thing in my
book,
as long as it's said with lips wet with honesty.

I prefer the dark truth over the grey lies anyway.

Save your lies, I don't want them,

the truth always saves me in the end.

When I tell you what hurts, please always
remember,
it's not to shine a flashlight at your imperfection,
it is not me challenging you to a blame game,
a pointing contest to see whose finger has the
most dirt.
I promise you it's not to put our hands over each
other's mouths to suffocate our truths.
It's to make sure we don't become drunk on
assumptions and let them drive us to crash what
we are building.

I don't want it to be another try with you.

I don't want to be another page in your story.

I've grown tired of trying.

And I am looking for someone who's not
looking just to try, but to build with me.

The best way to convince me to separate from
certain things for the sake of our relationship
is to keep showing me that you do not have your
heart hidden from me.

Love may be for those who seek it, but it's not a
game of hide-and-seek.

I am not afraid of compromising,
I'm just not willing to sacrifice another thing for
something with a short expiration date.

I will not be a savior to you nor do
I possess the power to erase the pain.

I am here to love you with a love that
will help the memories of your pain die slowly.

I don't want to keep predicting our downfall.
I don't want to keep trying to find lies in your
truth.
I don't want to keep trying to look for the
heartbreak that hasn't happened.
I don't want to keep holding on to my addiction to
pessimism.

I want to see the best in us and keep my eyes
there.
I want to stand on trust.
I want to keep my heartbreaks from breaking our
hearts.
I want to be positive about something good once
again.

Arguments and disagreements scare me.

I've learned to avoid conflict just so they never
show their face in my relationships.

My reality has always been that they show up like
the grim reaper.

The death of the relationship is always followed
by their presence.

I have learned to be sensitive enough,
to let love flow in and out of me,
but not sensitive enough to become
a child to my emotions,
and a punching bag for anyone's opinions.

Promise me you will not leave when I change for the better and that you will not use, "You changed" as the clause to breach this love contract I've signed with my heart.

There's no devil on the details here, you'll only find a commitment to growth when you read between the lines.

Please don't let apologies
become how we fix things,
but how we find what needs fixing.

Know that I will not hesitate to leave if I keep
finding reasons to.

Being fooled enough taught me to call a spade a
spade before it cuts me.

I am still trying to find the meaning of this life,
I am still learning to trust myself,
I am still learning my own worth.
There is nothing more I need from anyone but
patience and eyes that do not judge my bad days.

Despite me favoring consistency over loyalty,
I still like my grass watered with it.

Stand by my side even when the worst is in front
of us
and I will have your back whether the good comes
or not.

There are no more calendar days open for me to make myself available for anyone who cannot be emotionally available anymore.

Digging for love in a closed heart is a crime I will not keep committing against myself.

The 'don't worry, we're just friends' has never
been a safety net, but a knife I've fallen on with
nothing to grab hold of to save me.

They may just be friends, but those words have
been more stop signs for me, so I yield when they
start to fall from the lips I've kissed.

Good friendships are never the enemy, but in a
promiscuous world of people playing with hearts,
being cautious is only wise.

I will not try to convince you I am the best lover.

I can only prove to you that
I will love you the best way I can.

Be patient with me.

Pain has been the only one slow to leave me,

unlike everyone else.

When trust isn't there,

suggestions become chains of controls,

accountability becomes curse words,

and love looks like a story of fantasy

that will soon fade into reality.

Seeing eye-to-eye is almost impossible

when love isn't being seen.

The no's that keep coming out of my mouth for
certain things are my way of protecting myself.
I've said 'yes' so often that now I sometimes have
to say, 'no' to compensate.
I say, 'no' to balance it all out.
This is why some of my no's may mean 'yes' and
the yeses are just me returning to old habits.

If it feels like I focus too much on making sure you
know me,
I think that's the only thing that will keep you
from leaving.
Unfortunately, everyone I've gotten to know the
real version of, leaves.
I don't want you on that list.
If you get to know me and choose to stay, I
promise I'll be able to finish your sentences.

People don't just fall out of love.
Either little things add up and they slowly break
away, or they were never in love in the first place.
I am seeing the big picture with us,
don't miss the smaller things that matter to me.

My boundaries are not to keep you away,
they are to keep me from falling into an unknown
I've tasted before,
the experience that felt like fiberglass chewing on
my heart.

Boundaries keep me from skipping my way into
something good but walking into it instead,
the boundaries are for me, but also for you to
show me that you are what I've been searching
for.

I am not looking for happiness inside of you,
I am looking for commitment and reasons to never
have to protect my heart from you.

I've been single so long that being in a relationship
with myself has become the norm.

I must admit, you are competing against someone
for me,
you are in competition with *me* for me.

I know I can be biased and unfair, but I promise
you I am slowly learning to share myself with
someone else.

Although I've broken my own heart plenty of
times, I am the only one who truly never meant to.

It's hard to see red flags when people only show
things that will get your heart to throw the white
flag and surrender to what looks promising.

A manipulative trick to convince hearts to consent
to abuse uses their true nature to love.

If you ever wonder why people like me end up
with exes like that,
it's because we were fooled by the best of fools
and their magic.

I have seen so many beautiful love stories turn
ugly when the filters are off,
relationship goals that never reached their goal,
couples showing the world a love that doesn't
exist in their world.

Everything on my timeline is here to stay,
you will as well,
when you stay.

I am not desperate for love,
I am in need of it.
I am convinced we aren't meant to survive
being our own lovers in this life.

Self-love is good but to be in love while loving
yourself is amazingly great.

All that I've known of love is that it leaves, I have a
feeling you'll stay.
I want you to stay.
I will do everything for you to stay,
until your feelings have clearly checked out.

I am learning to let myself indulge in a love that
cups my face,
demands my eyes lock into its eyes,
and convinces me to not look back.

Because looking back to see if there's more,
something better or if something is missing,
is how many lose sight of gratitude for what they
have and let it go.

Don't let me feel alone,
don't let loneliness be the one I cheat with.

Don't let it be what cheats us
of our potential and our growth.

I do not need a savior,
I've accepted Jesus Christ into my life
as my Lord and Savior.

I am not looking for someone to worship for
giving me grace.

I don't need someone to praise for accepting me.

I am after the love I've prayed for and a lover who
is flawed, yet perfect for me.

My wishes,

their disappointment,

their promises,

my blind expectations,

have always been one in the same.

I rely on potential

while they fail to come close

to the ones I have of them.

Water my soul
with words
that reinforce
you are here,
that you are listening,
that you have roots
running to our foundation.

Tell me about who stole your smile.
Maybe it'll help me surrender mine at the sound of
your name.

Tell me about the rejection you've met on the path
to love.
Maybe it'll help me accept you with open arms.

Tell me about the things you never told anyone
else,
maybe they will help me believe that you are not
anyone else.

Tell me how they failed you
and maybe it'll become the blueprint for how our
relationship succeeds.

I've prepared my wedding day so many times that
now it has become my national break-up day.
I don't mind talking about marriage but until we
are there, my feet will always be cold.

Sometimes I wonder, maybe they deserved me,
but they didn't know how to nurture my soul.
To compensate, they fled instead of running to the
responsibilities that come with loving me head on.
I must admit, I've walked away from good
relationships before.
Sabotaging what could've been with my
immaturity.

Mistakes I will never make again, yet the truth
stands that I've been guilty of running away from
the very thing I desired.
I have met those who didn't deserve me, but also
those I did not deserve and those who I failed to
serve the love I should've shared with them.

Being patient with me is not tolerating me.
As someone who has seen more horror shows
than love movies,
I am learning the two aren't the same.

I am holding my heart in pieces because,
though I am whole enough,
I cannot stretch my hand and dump those pieces
into yours.
I'm only capable of sharing it piece-by-piece until
the entire thing rests in your palms.

Happiness knows my name.
It has lived in my bones before,
it rented my smile before,
it knows my soul.
When you don't see its presence on my face,
just know I am calling it home.

I will never make excuses for the way I hide my
heart and tell you to find it,
the way I play hide-and-seek with my feelings,
the way I push back on affection while begging for
you to pull it in.

I'm guilty of the inconsistencies I've condemned in
others, that I've barked at and fought against.

The difference between me and them is that I
genuinely want to put my guard down.

Being punched in the heart too many times has
made defending it the way to love myself.

My contradictions are a cry for help, a cry for
understanding, a whisper to look deeper.

I am not making excuses, I am making it clear that
I am fearfully inconsistent, but never a hypocrite
on purpose.

The right words have always found the wrong way
to leave my lips.
I have always wanted the ears of my lovers to hear
how I truly felt,
but for so long, my words were unwelcomed,
misinterpreted, and disregarded.
Over time, voicing my frustration became one of
the loudest ways I expressed myself.

I will never make it my duty
to make sure you are faithful.
I only believe I am responsible
for treating you like no one else
has treated you.

If that cannot keep you faithful,
then you and I are not meant to be.

There will be some uncertainty walking in our
midst, making my tongue heavy when I say 'no' to
some things.
I am unsure how to say certain things.
I am not indecisive,
I am just learning to trust myself, to put my needs
first.
Please don't take it as a sign that all my NOs are
the same.
Just know that when my NO sounds like a yes,
it's me struggling inside to find the words.
We don't all easily climb from under the rumble of
the pieces of a broken heart,
some of us lay under the hurt too long,
some of us find the broken pieces too heavy to
push off,
some simply just dust off the experience and
march on.
Those of us who need more strength aren't
weaker.

I am a full-time lover.
Love to me is a process,
a slow progression.
Every day I wake up,
get dressed,
and get ready to labor for the same heart,
working different angles to get the job done.
If there is anything I pride myself on,
it's that every part of you will get more
than enough overtime from me.

Be considerate.

I've been overlooked for too long.

Consider my feelings.

Consider my words.

Consider my effort.

Consider my needs.

Consider my existence

and everything in between.

Slowly freeing myself,

pulling apart the weeds,

suffocating this green field of my heart.

The field has known drought when it comes to

love, but the grass never died,

It has been unfertilized and unwatered,

neglected with every chance.

Despite this, I am doing my best to keep it green

and invite you to join me.

Loving <u>You</u>

Love me right and I will write thousands of poems about loving you.

I am praying in this lifetime, I get to love who you
were before your heart got cracked,
before that first promise was fumbled,
before your innocence was left floating on oceans
of tears.

I am praying that I get to taste such love from you.
Loving you as you are is beautiful,
but I am aching for something deep.
I just want a taste of something so magical,
unexplainable, something that feels familiar, yet
I've never experienced.

Let's create beautiful memories that will bury the
nightmare of experience we have known.
Let's find new roots to help our love blossom into
an oak tree that will stand forever.

All I want
is for you
to love me during the days
I need it most.

Let your untold story fall unto my ears.

Let your scars find their voice in my presence.

Let your desires find refuge on my chest.

Let your heart fall into my hands.

Let your mind open up to me for exploration.

Let yourself be mine, for I am yours.

To be honest, I am not worried about loving
you the way you ought to be loved.

How can a person even figure that out?

My only intent is to love you the best way
I know how to and pray that is enough.

I will love you so loud that your insecurities pack
up and move far away from us!

I am coming undone for you, undressing the
sacred parts, giving every drop of me to you.
Love without risk is a fairytale that doesn't come
with reward.
I want to surrender every bit of me for every bit of
you in return.
I am ready, I am naked, I am willing to be
wholeheartedly yours.

Bathe me with your love.
I have always thirsted for love, yet fearful to
drown in one where the deepest part of it carries a
monster that would take my life.

Bathe me with your love, now that I know it is
safe.
I don't need the life jacket.
I don't need the swimming goggles.
I don't need the air.
I want to drown in you, see all that you are, and
breathe in every drop of your love.

Sweet nothings are all I've known.
A mouthful of cavities
and a bittersweet idea of what love can be.
But, you came with sweet everythings
on your lips,
showing me the difference between salt and sugar.

When your nights get lonely, I want you to
remember you aren't alone.

When your days get difficult, I want you to know I
will walk into tomorrow with you.

When the darkness is too thick, just know I will
help you make a way through.

You don't have to walk your journey alone
anymore, I am looking to do life with you.

Your vulnerability gives mine the courage to speak
loudly.
Being an open book allows my stories to be told.
Being emotionally available has opened the door
for my feelings to breathe.
Letting people in is sometimes the best way to
teach them how to let you in.

Let's not speak to each other in tension and let
silence become our favorite language.

Instead, let's let our heart carry beautiful
conversations, and let grace and understanding
never leave our lips.

I don't want to be closed to you
I want to be close to you.

Make me feel like I exist,
like your eyes never turned from me.

I don't need to feel wanted, I want to feel needed.

The rumors they spin about you are their
opinions. I want to know the truth from your
mouth and judge you for your true character. I
want to shine the flashlight on your intentions and
see who lives under those flaws.
I cannot count yesterday's shortcomings, I can
only keep an eye on today and see how we can
grow with one another tomorrow.

I don't need to wake up with your name glowing on my phone screen everyday or gifts at my doorsteps every week.

I am not after a bunch of grand gestures that will gather likes from people passing time on Instagram.

I want you to consistently be here, your presence to remain on the timeline of my life.

I want what can be felt more than it can be seen.

I will learn to see your flowers as gifts instead of apologies.

I will remind myself that your gifts are presents instead of a way to stall my absence.

I will tell myself that your presence is not here to fade into overstayed tension and arguments tossed into baskets of grudges.

I will see you differently, as long as you don't stop being different.

The way your hand found the perfect way to hold
my heart has been helping me play love songs to
drown out the voice of self-doubt.

When you said it, I felt a sudden fear,
it was no different than what I often feel
when a plane begins to lower its altitude,
slowly descending as it gets nearer to its
destination.

You dropped 'I love you' on me at a time
my head was no longer in the clouds,
it has yet to land on my conscience.

I've given too many deaf ears to those
words to easily accept them.
Please give me a little time,
I'll say it back and mean it.

I am not used to having someone who is such a
perfect match,
someone who is on fire for me the way I have a
burning desire for them.

I am not used to my awkwardness being
entertainment.
I am not used to being heard like this.
I am not used to feeling seen beyond my flesh.
I am not used to that many things being brought to
the table.

The world may have caused
me to be cold,
but your love,
I will let melt
everything inside of me.

I've been guilty of loving
too hard and too little.

Loving too hard taught me to ease
up a little and loving too little reminded
me that loving too hard is needed.

Keep the promises that you don't see yourself
keeping tucked inside your mind,
buried down your throat with all your unspoken
words.

Unintentionally lying is one of the most subtle
ways to start destroying trust.

In your presence,
I love being naked and vulnerable.
The version of me the
public knows is washed off,
the version of me friends know
is taken off and put aside.
With you, I am a completely naked soul.
I am not fake with other people,
they just do not get to see certain parts of me.
Those parts I've grown more than
comfortable showing you.

I've been searching for you.
I have searched in the lovers who
came before you, during the times
my heart fought pain with a bloody fist.
I searched for you when I began to
believe I was love-repellent.
I have been searching for love that only
you can carry for someone like me.

I shouldn't have to tell you
that those words hurt,
you should see it in my shaky eyes
and how discomfort flows through my body
after they've settled themselves into my eardrums.
But if I have to tell you,
please listen without having a response on
the tip of your tongue ready to jump the gun.

I am an emotional mess
learning to give rainbows a home.

Love lives here now.
It took it awhile to find my address
while I moved from heart-to-heart
calling too many lovers "home."
Since I stopped searching for it in people,
it came here and asked me to make this
vessel a permanent home.

I promise I am different.
I must say I've been terrible
at keeping promises before,
but this one is easy to keep.
If anything,
promise not to treat me
any different than you treated the
first person you ever fell for.

Love isn't meant to be bittersweet.
It is meant to be sweet on most occasions
and salt to a wound on others.

I used to be a 'let's test the waters' type of lover.
If it was cold, I ran,
if it warmed me up enough, I stayed.
I am no longer this way.
I am an all-or-nothing lover.
I'm here to stay whether it's red hot or freezing
cold.
As long as it doesn't freeze my heart,
I will fight.
I am a lover who is looking to stay.

I am here for lasting promises,
promising forever,
forever field of memories,
memories that never end,
ending thirsts,
thirst for trust,
trusting love,
love's safety,
safely lasting beyond promises.

Give me passage,
grant me permission to be in your presence,
to flow through your mind,
and dance to the fading end of your heartaches.

Give me room in your life, I've opened my whole
soul for you to live in.

I've waited long enough for an authentic love, my
wish is that you are what I've waited this long for.

They say good things come to those who wait, I
am praying that with you, I am done waiting.

Together we can expand each other's vocabulary,
call each other new names that describe who we
are to one another,
find new ways to express.
Let's redefine relationships,
and give love new meanings.

I promise to hold your smile, to carry your heart
everywhere with me.

Pouring your love in empty cups with damaged
bottoms has been exhausting.

Whatever you pour into us will be enough.

There will be rest here and refills if you ever feel
empty.

Together, I want us to flow through each other,
like rivers connecting.

The drought will never know us.

I want to know your softeners, your fire, your
power, your conviction, your weaknesses, your
laughter, your mind, your resilience, your
magnitude more than I want to know your hands,
your lips, your eyes, your thighs, and everything in
between.

Allow me to live in your depth, where the roots
talk and I can explore every corner of your mind.

Correct me when I am wrong,
it's only the mature thing to do,
but when you do,
please butter up the words with grace,
serve a side of understanding with it,
leave the anger uncooked,
maybe add a little "Honey" in the opening
sentence.
Please don't serve it cold.
I may like my morning coffee black,
but not at the wrong temperature.
No one wants to wake up to a sloppy breakfast.

There are countless relationships that are toxic
simply because both partners are unheard.
They exchange with each other without
communication being a building block.
The foundation is never prepared enough for
apologies, for comprehension, for listening.
Too many people are trying to grow flowers from
the concrete instead of creating a garden to
cultivate one another.

Let's play this game.
Whoever admits their wrongs first collects kisses.
Whoever says, "I love you," first wins a devoted
heart.
The person who shares the deepest things about
themselves gets unlimited support.

Let's play a game where we both win.

I am willing to love you under one condition.
Under the condition that your love doesn't stay
conditional.

I know we have to ease our way into becoming
boundaryless.

We must grow our way into full surrender, but
promise me that conditions will not remain the
gatekeeper.

I'm here to handle your storm, to walk through the
rain with you,
to be your calm when you are a tornado,
I will not drown when you are a tsunami washing
whatever comes your way.
I will walk with my chest out and my heart bare
even if your mouth rains hail.
As long as you don't leave me when the rainbow
comes and move your love to another town when
your sky is blue.

Treat me as your equal,
being on pedestals require me to look down to
you,
and being treated with less makes it harder for me
to look up to you.
We belong at the same level whether we are above
or under, all that matters is that we are hand-in-
hand walking into love.

I am no longer holding my breath,
waiting for unexpected to happen,
something to go wrong.

You belong to me, I belong to you.

We belong to each other.

You belong to you and I belong to me.

We also belong to ourselves.

Loving me right will be an act of bravery, just as
loving myself has been.
It will be a journey of emotions escaping bottles
and heart spills on surfaces where slip-and-falls
have no warning signs.

There's a complexity in the simple act of
surrendering yourself into arms promising to love
you until last breaths come. Well-wishing that
often turns into wishing wells full of pocket
change and heart's desires without granted
wishes.

Loving me right comes as a walk through hell with
heaven as bait. It will not burn your soul but there
will be fire testing us, winter visiting us, and
doubtful tomorrow amongst us. Just like anything
good in this life, loving me will come with reward
but there will be risks, there will be sweat, there
will be sacrifices, as well as a lot of learning and
re-learning.

Loving me will not be easy but it will be real, it will
come with loving you, it will push through the

midnights, the rivers of tears, the ashes of old
memories.

Loving me will be worth it, so will loving you if
you choose to believe that we are worth it.

The End

Thank you for reading.

Let's connect:

Join my TEXT community: **+1 (239) 203-2991**

Listen to our podcast: **REALationship Therapy** (on all platforms)

Want to read more?

Free Book

Watering Your Soil

Download at **wateringyoursoil.com**

Best Sellers

HER

HER Vol. 2

Ashes of Her Love

Heal. Grow. Love.

Unspoken Feelings of a Gentleman

To the Women I Once Loved

HIM

Other Books

Sparking Her Own Flame

Unspoken Feelings of a Gentleman II

In Love with You

Apologies That Never Came

Really Moving On

All available at pierrejeanty.com

Need a Journal?

pierrejeanty.com/collections/journals

Want quotes & poetry on your wall?

pierrejeanty.com/collections/wallart

Drink coffee or tea?

pierrejeanty.com/collections/mugs

Want to wear your heart out?

https://pierrejeanty.com/collections/apparel

Let's be social

Tik Tok: **Pierreajeanty**

Instagram: **Pierrejeanty**

Twitter: **Pierreajeanty**